C000217503

Participating in the Mass

Celebrating the Liturgy
with dignity and beauty

By
Dom Cuthbert Johnson OSB

*All booklets are published thanks to the
generous support of the members of the
Catholic Truth Society*

CATHOLIC TRUTH SOCIETY
PUBLISHERS TO THE HOLY SEE

Contents

The Art of Celebration

"Let us seek to celebrate the Eucharist with ever deeper dedication and zeal." (Pope Benedict XVI)

The introduction of a new translation of the Roman Missal has been welcomed as a suitable occasion for renewed catechesis on the celebration of Mass. Many hope that this catechesis will lead to a rediscovery of an atmosphere of recollection and the sense of the mystery of God's presence in our midst which is sometimes lacking in our Liturgy. There is also a widespread desire to see more dignity and beauty in our liturgical celebrations.

To achieve this, ritual solemnity and a good aesthetic sense is not enough. Care for external details must be accompanied by attention to internal dispositions: "The gaze of my heart must be turned toward the Lord who is in our midst: this is what the art of celebration means and it is the proper way of celebrating." (*Pope Benedict XVI*)

The expression

To understand the meaning of the expression 'the art of celebration' in relation to the Liturgy it is necessary to clarify what is meant by 'art' and what is implied by 'celebration'.

Art should be understood here as the development of a skill or the mastery of a subject. This does not exclude the aesthetic dimension of art, but it is far more comprehensive. It is the acquisition of a habit of thinking, acting and doing in an orderly manner.

The fundamentals of a genuine 'art' of celebration are harmony and order. This what Pope Benedict means when he speaks of lifting up our hearts in the Liturgy. It is the harmony between what we say with our lips and what we think with our heart. We must raise our heart to the Lord, not only as a ritual response but as an expression of what is happening in this heart that is uplifted, and also lifts up others. "In other words, the 'art of celebration' is not intended as an invitation to some sort of theatrical performance, but to an interiority that makes itself felt and becomes acceptable and evident to the people taking part. Only if they see that this is not an exterior or spectacular 'art', but the expression of the journey of our heart that attracts their hearts too, will the Liturgy become beautiful, will it become the communion with the Lord of all who are present." (*Pope Benedict XVI*)

Celebration

Celebration as an art should not be confused with the art of presiding. The art of celebration is the concern of the whole congregation according to their different orders, functions, and actual participation (*General Instruction of the Roman Missal* (GIRM) n. 91).

Saint Peter's declaration that we are a chosen race, a royal priesthood, a holy nation, and Pope Saint Leo the Great's call: recognise your dignity, O Christian, are fundamental to our understanding of the art of celebration.

The scope and purpose of this study

"The liturgical prescriptions laid down by the Church are not external appendices but express in practice the reality of the revelation of Christ's Body and Blood." (Pope Benedict XVI)

This brief work is designed to make a contribution towards enhancing the dignity and beauty of the celebration of Mass. It is more than a list of directives on what to do and what not do in the celebration of the Liturgy. These matters will be dealt with only in so far as they contribute to the good order of the celebration.

The purpose of this study is to provide a liturgical and theological underpinning to the directives for celebrating the Liturgy. Without this the mere observance of ceremonial and rubrics will not foster that intelligent and active participation which is necessary for the sharing in the mystery of Christ through the sacred celebration of the Liturgy.

Rubrics

"For the preservation of good order and charity"
(Saint Benedict)

The first collections of liturgical texts contained only the prayers to be used in a given celebration. From the thirteenth century in particular there began to appear directives regarding the actions and gestures to accompany the words. To distinguish them from the prayer texts, which were in black ink, the directives were written or printed in red ink and came to be known as 'rubrics', from the Latin word for red, 'ruber'.

Rubrics are important in the measure in which they contribute to the preservation of good order and charity. Using a play upon words it might be said that rubrics safeguard the rights of Catholics to have the Rites as authorised by the Church.

"In the Eucharistic celebration we do not invent something but rather enter into a reality that precedes us, indeed that embraces Heaven and earth and therefore also past, future and present." (Pope Benedict XVI)

It is also true that certain aspects of the ceremonial can have an ethical dimension when they are related to issues such as justice, fairness and equality. A liturgical abuse risks being much more than an unauthorised or inappropriate modification of the Liturgy, for it can also be an abuse of the rights and dignity of both the priest and the people. (cf. *Redemptionis Sacramentum* (RS) n. 24).

"The faithful have a true right to participate in the liturgical celebrations as the Church wills and not according to the personal likes of a particular minister, nor according to unapproved and unusual rites, expressions of specific groups which tend to cut themselves off from the universality of the People of God." (*Directory on the Life and Ministry of Priests* (DLMP) n. 64)

"Worship God acceptably with reverence and awe" (Heb 12:28)

Rubrics have been a matter of concern for many decades. Long before the Second Vatican Council it was recognised that an excessive preoccupation with rubrics was not a healthy approach to the celebration of the Liturgy. The eminent liturgist Mgr Klaus Gamber, by no means a radical in his thought, described the Mass as then celebrated as "congealed and ossified by rubricism, rigidly controlled by the Congregation of Rites, long overdue for reform."

A similar observation was made by the then Father Joseph Ratzinger who, shortly before the publication of the Council's Decree on the Liturgy, wrote about "the dangerous archaism which had come to enshroud the

Mass since Trent, so that the real meaning of its various parts was no longer intelligible."

Renewal of the Liturgy

"An organic bond exists between the renewal of the Liturgy and the renewal of the whole life of the Church. The Church takes from the Liturgy the strength for life." (Pope Benedict XVI)

At the time of the Second Vatican Council, the Liturgy was being celebrated with care and a degree of splendour. In the academic world, liturgical journals were filled with learned studies to a standard which has not since been surpassed. Scholarly studies were being published which were the fruit of both a life spent in dedicated research and a lived experience of the Liturgy.

This was the background against which the Council Fathers held their discussions concerning the need for the renewal of the Liturgy. The Bishops remembered that Pope Pius XII had stated that: "in the Liturgy there are human elements as well as divine. The latter, obviously, having been established by our Redeemer, cannot under any circumstances be changed; but the human elements may be modified in various ways ... according as time, circumstances and the needs of souls demand." (Pope Pius XII, *Mediator Dei*, 54-55)

The work of liturgical renewal already had a long history. It began in the first half of the eighteenth century and led Blessed Pope Pius IX to attempt to revise the Calendar. Further work of renewal was undertaken under Pope Saint Pius X and Pope Pius XII. From the following words of Blessed Pope John XXIII, it would appear that even if the Second Vatican Council had not taken place, liturgical renewal would still have continued:

"in 1956, when preparatory studies were being conducted for a general liturgical reform, our predecessor decided to survey the opinions of the bishops on the liturgical improvement of the Roman Breviary. After duly weighing the answers of the bishops, he judged that it was time to attack the problem of a general and systematic revision of the rubrics of the Breviary and Missal. This question he referred to the special committee of experts who have been appointed to study the general liturgical reform. Then the problem became ours. After we had decided, under the inspiration of God, to convene an ecumenical council, we turned over in our mind what was to be done about this project begun by our predecessor. After mature reflection, we came to the conclusion that the more important principles governing a general liturgical reform should be laid before the members of the hierarchy at the forthcoming ecumenical council."
(*Blessed Pope John XXIII*, July 25, 1960)

It should be understood that the liturgical renewal of the Second Vatican Council was part of a development, and was not a break in tradition. Pope Benedict XVI has often drawn attention to the continuity of tradition and has insisted that what preceded the Council and what followed are a manifestation of the living tradition of the Church.

The Liturgy as a Work of Art

"Beauty is not mere decoration but rather an essential element of the liturgical action, since it is an attribute of God himself and his revelation." (Pope Benedict XVI)

The Liturgy of the Roman Rite is a notable and precious part of the liturgical treasure and patrimony of the Catholic Church (GIRM 397). The Liturgy is a precious work of art and to make arbitrary modifications to it should be as unthinkable as trying to improve the work of a great painter, sculptor or musician. The failure to recognise the Liturgy as a precious part of the patrimony of the Church has caused grave harm to the Church.

Neglect of the aesthetic aspect of the Liturgy can be detrimental to the faith, as Pope Benedict stated: "The relationship between creed and worship is evidenced in a particular way by the rich theological and liturgical category of beauty. Like the rest of Christian Revelation, the Liturgy is inherently linked to beauty: it is 'the splendour of truth'. The Liturgy is a radiant expression of the paschal mystery, in which Christ draws us to himself and calls us to communion". The theologian Hans Urs von Balthasar expressed the fear that the denial of beauty could lead to a Christian being "no longer capable of praying and, before long, not even of loving".

Much anguish and upset could have been avoided if the Council's exhortation had been followed: "that all things set apart for use in divine worship should be truly worthy, becoming, and beautiful, signs and symbols of the supernatural world." (*Sacrosanctum Concilium*, n. 122).

Signs and symbols

Christian symbolism must be understood in the light of the mystery of the Incarnation, as Pope Benedict XVI has declared: "The Incarnation means, in the first place, that the invisible God enters into the visible world, so that we, who are bound to matter, can know Him."

Through the mystery of the Incarnation, signs and symbols have taken on a new and more profound meaning. The greatest sign, the perfect Icon, is Christ Jesus who is, as Saint Paul tells us, the image of the invisible God. The Preface of Christmas draws our attention to this, by stressing that in Christ we see our God made visible and so are drawn to the love of things unseen. In former times, the Christian faithful had a great knowledge of signs and symbols. They understood and could interpret the stained glass windows and sculptures in great medieval cathedrals and churches. There is a real need today for teaching about symbolism and images drawn from Sacred Scripture.

"The beauty of the Liturgy is a sublime expression of God's glory" (Pope Benedict XVI)

Care for the aesthetics of religion is a reflection and a manifestation of the faith of a community. It is an unfortunate fact that the standard of the liturgical art to be found in many churches is not very high. The reason for this lies in the fact that sacred art has been turned into mere religious art. We can learn much from the icon painter of the Eastern church who fasts and prays before beginning the work, and anoints the materials with holy oil.

The decline in the quality of sacred art is a matter of concern to Pope Benedict XVI, who recognises that: "today we are experiencing not just a crisis of sacred art, but a crisis of art in general".

The feeble quality of some modern sacred images and much repository art does not give witness to the demanding, total self-giving and heroic virtue of the Christian life. The strength of truth and the power of love should find expression in sacred art. The beauty of holiness should be reflected in the quality and dignity of such work. Works of sacred art should evoke the deepest and noblest aspirations of the Christian soul and give edification to the unbeliever. Edification is a word which is little heard of today and yet much needed. All sacred art must remind us that nothing can separate us from the love of Christ, the following of whom demands that we take up our cross and seek to enter by the narrow way that leads to eternal life.

All sacred images are, without exception, in a certain sense images of the Resurrection, history read in the light of the Resurrection, and for that very reason they are images of hope, giving us the assurance of the world to come, of the final coming of Christ (*Pope Benedict XVI*).

Recent Popes from Paul VI to Benedict XVI have called upon artists to put their God given talents at the service of the faith: "Let the beauty that you express by your God-given talents always direct the hearts of others to glorify the Creator, the source of all that is good." (*Pope Benedict XVI*)

Christian artists must be encouraged and to do this they must be commissioned to make works of sacred art for our churches and religious houses. It is time to put an end to cheap and tasteless posters and banners and to ensure that beauty is restored to worship in form, colour and sound. Art can help recall that in a world of action contemplation is necessary and that there is "a path of beauty which is at the same time an artistic and aesthetic journey, a journey of faith, of theological enquiry." (*Pope Benedict XVI*)

The Setting for the Celebration of the Liturgy

"Beauty, like truth, brings joy to the human heart"
(Pope Paul VI)

Art and architecture in the context of the Liturgy are inseparable. If Liturgy is the language of the Church, then art, music and architecture are important parts of her vocabulary. The architectural setting for the celebration of the Liturgy must be a reflection of the Liturgy which is celebrated within it.

The quality of the work and materials used in the reordering of churches in the two decades following the Second Vatican Council was commendable, but it is now recognised that some arrangements need to be re-examined.

The words of the psalmist should readily come to mind on entering a church: "How lovely is your dwelling place, O Lord." Clearly such sentiments are hardly possible when the entrance area is cluttered with posters, leaflets, newsletters and stacked chairs.

Saint Benedict declared in his Rule for monks that the church should be a place which is conducive to prayer: *"Let the oratory be what its name implies, and let nothing else be done or kept there."*

The primary manifestation of beauty in a church is its good order and cleanliness. The beauty which is fitting to the house of the Lord does not need to be lavish nor ostentatious. The following observation taken from the diary of Cardinal Bellarmine (1542-1621) is worth noting:

"Near the end of my journey, I enjoyed the hospitality of a Bishop of noble birth and considerable fortune. His palace was resplendent with vessels of silver, his table covered with rich ware, table linen and everything else was immaculately clean, the whole creating a most pleasant atmosphere. But on the following day, as I came down to the church at a very early hour to celebrate Mass, I met a complete contrast. Everything was base and repugnant, so much so that I hardly dared celebrate the holy Mysteries in such a place, with such lack of ornament."

Over one hundred years later, in 1749, Pope Benedict XIV felt the need to draw attention to the same matter: "We recommend with all our strength and above all: that churches should be very well kept decorated, should be clean, and furnished with all the necessary sacred objects. We do not intend, with these words, to insist on sumptuous or magnificent accoutrements for holy buildings, nor on rich or expensive furnishings; we are aware these are not everywhere possible; what we wish is decency and cleanliness. These can co-exist with poverty, and can be adapted to it; no one can object to our requiring these." (*Annus qui hunc*, February 19, 1749)

"Everything should be done in a fitting and orderly way" (1 Cor 14: 40)

What Pope Pius XII said in 1947 is still important:

"We desire to commend and urge the adornment of churches and altars. Let each one feel moved by the inspired word, 'the zeal of thy house has eaten me up'; and strive as much as possible to ensure that everything in the church, including vestments and liturgical furnishings, even though not rich nor lavish, be perfectly clean and appropriate, since all is consecrated to the Divine Majesty. If we have previously disapproved of the error of those who would wish to outlaw images from churches on the plea of reviving an ancient tradition, We now deem it Our duty to censure the inconsiderate zeal of those who propose for veneration in the Churches and on the altars, without any just reason, a multitude of sacred images and statues, and also those who display unauthorized relics, those who emphasize special and insignificant practices, neglecting essential and necessary things. They thus bring religion into derision and lessen the dignity of worship." (*Mediator Dei*, n. 189)

Not all church communities can afford works of art, but all can acquire the art of good order and cleanliness. It should be remembered that the sacristy is not a store room, it is the place where the immediate preparations for the sacred Liturgy take place, and this should be reflected in its furnishings and maintenance. Its atmosphere should help those who are preparing for the celebration to do so in silence and recollection.

"The Church is nourished by the bread of life which she finds at the table both of the Word of God and the body of the Lord".

The altar

The sacrifice of the Cross is made present on the altar which is also the Lord's table to which the faithful are invited to share the bread of life and the cup of eternal salvation. The altar is a sign of the Church's twofold activity of the worship of God and our sanctification.

The church is built for the altar, and the altar must never be treated as merely one of the more important parts of the church's furnishings.

When the altar is anointed with holy chrism, it becomes a sign of the Anointed One, our Lord Jesus Christ, who is the victim, priest and altar of his own life-giving sacrifice. Through the invocation of the Holy Spirit, the altar becomes a sign of the saving work of Christ our Lord. The altar is always the silent yet eloquent witness to the saving work of our Mediator with the Father, Christ Jesus our High Priest.

The altar is a sign of eternal life, for from it we receive the food which is the pledge of future glory. It is through sharing in this sacred table that the assembled people of God discover their identity as God's chosen people, the new Israel, and become bearers of the message of salvation for the whole world.

For over a thousand years of the Church's history, devotion to the altar was an important part of Catholic piety. The faithful went to the altar with their prayers of petition, praise and thanksgiving. There is a need to encourage this understanding of the place of the altar in the spiritual life of the faithful. Rightly understood, devotion to the altar is one of the more deeply theological devotions of the Christian people. This teaching is embodied in the prayer which follows the Litany of the Saints in the *Rite of the Dedication of an Altar*: "May this altar be the place where the great mysteries of redemption are accomplished: a place where your people offer their gifts, unfold their good intentions, pour out their prayers, and echo every meaning of their faith and devotion."

The sanctuary is a holy place because of the presence of the altar, around which the whole worshipping community is gathered. It is only correct to speak of the sanctuary as a place set apart when this is understood as set apart for the altar and not set apart from the people.

The placing of the Christmas crib in front of the altar is not allowed. Nor should the altar should be decorated or surrounded with plants and flowers at any time in such a way as to obscure its dignity and function. Pictures, even icons, should not be placed on the altar or resting up against it.

The ambo

The wealth and variety of biblical readings is appreciated by all of God's people. The sacred and sacramental character of the place and the book from which the Word of God is proclaimed needs to be explained.

In the ancient basilicas the ambo, both in its structure and it's positioning, proclaimed its character as an integral part of the celebration of the Liturgy. It was often carefully decorated to underline its importance and to show it to be a throne for the word of God; it both symbolised the table of the word and the seat of wisdom.

The ambo is for the proclamation of the Word of God, which includes the responsorial psalm. It may also be used for the homily and the Prayer of the Faithful.

It is not to be used as a music desk. The cantor, the conductor of the choir or of the assembly, and the commentator should all use a moveable stand or lectern.

The ambo is truly regarded as the table of God's word in the same way in which the altar is the table of the Lord's body and blood.

The two tables

The image of the two tables, the table of Word of God and the table of the Eucharist, is found in the teaching of the great Fathers of the Church. St Augustine declared, "from the table of the Lord we receive the bread of life... And from the table of Sunday readings we are nourished with the doctrine of the Lord" (*Commentary on Psalm* 127, 10).

This teaching is also found for example in the great classic of the Middle Ages, *The Imitation of Christ*: "there are two tables placed among the treasures of the Church. One is the table of the holy altar on which rests a consecrated bread, the precious body of Jesus Christ. The other is the table of the divine Law. This contains the holy doctrine of the true faith, which lifts the veil of the sanctuary and leads us securely into the very Holy of holies." (Book 4, ch.11).

"Do you want to know what the Bible is? If you want to have some idea, look at the Tabernacle. What do you see? The Word of God Incarnate under the species of bread and wine as food for our souls. Look now at the Bible; what do you see? The Divine Word, the wisdom of the Father, who speaks to us therein until the end of time. There, He is truly present, a real presence. The Lord gives himself to us under two aspects; he gives us himself to teach us in the Holy Scriptures; he gives us himself to nourish us in the Eucharist. The two mysteries are complementary; the Church does not offer the Holy Sacrifice without the accompaniment of readings drawn from the Old and the New Testament; these readings are designed to indicate this double presence: the real substantial presence in the divine Host, and the presence no less real in the Scriptures." (Abbot Prosper Guéranger, *Retreat notes*, 1863).

The chair

The Eucharist is the action of Christ and the people of God, hierarchically assembled.

The president's chair should signify his office. The meaning of the Latin word 'to preside' means 'to sit in front of someone'. The one who presides must be able to communicate with the people, and this means more than just being seen and heard.

When the priest stands at the altar and offers the "holy and living sacrifice" his role is ontologically different from that when he is leading the people in prayer, or listening to the Word of God seated on his chair and explaining it in the homily.

The president's chair is a sign of his ministry of service in imitation of the Lord, who came not to be served but to serve and give himself for us through his sacrificial death and glorious Resurrection.

Liturgical dress

The artistic quality of liturgical vestments is without doubt in need of improvement. As the Cistercian monks of the twelfth century already recognised, there can be great nobility and beauty in the simplicity of material and the design of vestments. Saint Benedict, although not fashion conscious, insisted that the monk's "garments be not too short for their wearers, but of the proper fit". He did not want his monks to look well dressed but still he did not want them to look ill clad. The poor quality of the liturgical dress of some ministers is a matter of concern.

Dress is not something limited only to the ministers, the people, too, need to be reminded that they are going to the banquet of the Lord and should dress appropriately. Our standards should not be less than is expected and even demanded in civic buildings and restaurants.

Respect for others means that we do not just do what suits us, as Saint Benedict put it, "think first what is for the good of another before what is for your own good" - surely a key to a right understanding of peace and harmony.

Religious priests whose habit is white may not on this account omit the wearing of an alb.

Position of hands

The importance and significance of the position of hands during the celebration of the Liturgy should not be disregarded. The hands are recognised to be a most expressive part of the body. Hands can display happiness, showing approval or betray anxiety and nervousness.

To stretch out one's hands shows openness and a willingness to accept. We speak of taking the hand of friendship. It is accepted that in many spheres of life and work, body language is a help to understanding something of an individual's state of mind and well being. While restlessness shows itself in fidgeting, it is recognised that joining one's hands is therapeutic and a help towards concentration.

To join one's hands in the traditional gesture of prayer is helpful and conducive to recollection. Even the non-Christian spirituality of the East attaches great importance to the position of the hands in prayer and meditation.

Cultural differences bring different practices regarding postures for prayer, and postures for listening, but the important element common to all cultures is that gestures and postures unite the assembly, delineate areas of responsibility, facilitate participation and manifest the unity of the community.

Music in the Liturgy

"Let the word of Christ dwell in you abundantly, in all wisdom; teaching and admonishing one another in psalms, hymns; and spiritual canticles, singing with grace in your hearts to God." (Col 3: 16)

The Gospel tells us that at the end of the Last Supper the Lord and his disciples sang before leaving the upper room where they had celebrated the Passover Meal to go to the garden of Gethsemane. The example of the Lord and his disciples shows us that singing should be an integral part of our celebration of the Liturgy.

The first Christian communities were instructed by Saint Paul to praise the Lord with "psalms, hymns and spiritual songs". The first followers of Jesus, being from a Jewish background, were familiar with the psalms and canticles of Holy Scripture.

Sacred, Liturgical or religious music: what is the difference?

Music which has been composed specifically for the celebration of Divine Worship belongs to the category of sacred or liturgical music. Such music should minister to the sacred texts, whether they are drawn from Scripture or belong to the Church's patrimony of liturgical texts. New texts may be composed, but they should have the approval of the competent ecclesiastical authority so that they can become part of the Church's heritage.

Music composed for the Liturgy must serve to highlight, clarify, emphasise and underline elements of the sacred text. The melodic line should facilitate the participation of all present so that with one harmonious voice praise is given the Most Holy Trinity.

Music is an integral part of the celebration of the Liturgy and the musical tradition of the Church is "a treasure of great price".

Religious music

In the category of religious music are those compositions which have been inspired by texts of sacred Scripture or the Liturgy but were not intended for liturgical use. Even though such texts may have religious connotations or even direct reference to the Blessed Virgin Mary or the Saints, they may not be suitable for Liturgical use.

As regards instrumental music, solo or orchestral, the musical directive 'andante religioso' is purely aesthetical and does not necessarily qualify a musical composition as suitable for use in church.

While such restrictions might appear severe, this is not so. The restriction, far from being a limitation, is designed to encourage composers to put their gifts at the service of the Liturgy. To have to draw on 'secular religious music' is a sign of the cultural impoverishment which has inflicted the Church in many places during the past forty years.

Music at Mass

The Church desires that there should be some music and singing at all Masses celebrated with the assembled People of God. This is not an impossible ideal and it can become a reality even in those places that are limited in their musical resources.

Singing the acclamations after the consecration and the 'Great Amen' at the conclusion of the Eucharistic Prayer should be possible. Simple chants for the 'Holy, Holy' and the 'Lamb of God' are now available and are within the capability of most parishes.

The desire for simple melodies is praiseworthy, but the simplicity must be a noble one and exclude mediocre, banal and tuneless melodies.

If the people are to be encouraged to sing at Mass, the sacred ministers must lead the way by example. The Bishop, Priest and Deacon must sing the parts of the Liturgy which are proper to them. What Pope Benedict XVI asked of Bishops, applies in principle to all who exercise a liturgical ministry: "I would ask that every effort be made to ensure that the Liturgies which the Bishop celebrates in his Cathedral are carried out with complete respect for the art of celebration so that they can be considered an example for the entire Diocese."

Those celebrants who show care in their gestures and other sacred actions are teaching by example, and are giving what Saint Benedict calls "a twofold teaching, displaying all goodness and holiness by deeds and by words, but by deeds rather than by words."

Even when a choir is unavailable, a small schola of three or four singers can make a considerable contribution by sustaining the singing and so encouraging participation.

The benefit that can be brought to the Liturgy by a well-trained choir cannot be underestimated. As Pope Benedict XVI pointed out, a choir can contribute to developing "the sense of prayer, of dignity and of beauty" in the Liturgy. It may be necessary to allocate part of the parish budget to choir formation, and it will always be money well spent.

Hymns at Mass

Although hymns have played a significant role in promoting congregational singing, their place during Mass calls for careful consideration. While hymns are an integral part of the Protestant worship tradition, they have a different role to play in Catholic liturgical celebrations. The hymns of the Liturgy of the Hours are closely linked to the times of the Liturgical Year, to the Mystery or Feast being celebrated and even to the time of day. The introduction of poems and other texts into the English Liturgy of the Hours at first sight may have appeared attractive, but liturgically it was an impoverishment and a wrong turn.

If hymns are to be used at Mass, they should be chosen according to the occasion and should closely reflect the texts which are set for the day. There is need of a criteria to guide the choice of hymns. Some collections of hymns, often published without the approval of the competent authority, contain pieces which are quite unsuitable for a mature Christian community.

The texts for use at Mass

For over a century, the Church has appealed to the faithful not to sing at Mass but to sing the Mass. This appeal still makes sense. Before any thought is given to hymn singing or the introduction of anthems, the texts of the Mass should be sung. These texts are the Entrance Chant, the *Lord, have mercy*, the *Glory to God in the highest*, the Acclamations, the *Holy, Holy, Holy*, the *Lamb of God* and the Communion Antiphon.

The *Lord, have mercy*, the *Glory to God in the highest*, the Acclamations, the *Holy, Holy, Holy*, the *Lamb of God* must all be sung according to the approved text in the Missal, not altered in order to accommodate weak melodies.

Should the need arise to replace the Entrance Antiphon or Communion Antiphon by a hymn or anthem, care should be taken that the choice reflects the words and meaning of the Missal text. For example, the Communion Antiphon for the Solemnity of the Assumption is taken from the Canticle of Mary, the *Magnificat* (Luke 1: 48-49). This does not mean that any Marian hymn can be sung to replace it. Rather, a replacement hymn or anthem must reflect the words or sentiments of the *Magnificat*.

Liturgical music

The Holy Spirit who has given the gifts of great artists to the Church can in our times grant similar gifts. To deny this or to say that past forms of art or music can never be surpassed would be to limit the power of the Holy Spirit.

The Church has never declared any era of her history, any style or art form as the ideal nor has the Church ever proposed that an attempt be made to reproduce it.

Gregorian Chant is a precious part of the Church's patrimony and, as Pope Benedict XVI has said, is a model that can serve to inspire the composers of every age. Liturgical music ministers to the word and Gregorian chant has a unique and indispensable role in helping composers by providing a sublime model for inspiration.

There are many suitable Gregorian Chant Masses, such as Mass XIV and XV and Credo I which are accessible to the people. The Graduale simplex and the collection Jubilate Deo provide a worthy selection from the Gregorian repertoire.

The musical tradition of the Church contains many works which because of their complexity are reserved to a choir of trained singers. Such musical compositions still have their place in the Liturgy. A choir does not hinder the active participation of the people, as has sometimes erroneously been suggested. To listen is also a form of active participation and indeed is a requisite preliminary to all true participation.

The Organ

The organ is the most suitable instrument for use in the Liturgy. The organ should "accompany and sustain the singing either of the assembly or the choir. It must never be used to accompany the Prayers or chants of the celebrant nor the readings proclaimed by the reader or the deacon. In accordance with tradition, the organ should remain silent during penitential seasons, during Advent and the Liturgy for the Dead unless it is needed to support the singing. It is fitting that the organ be played before and after a celebration as a preparation and conclusion of the celebration. It is of considerable importance that in all churches there should be trained musicians and instruments of good quality. Care should be given to the maintenance of organs and respect shown towards their historical character both in form and tone." (Concerts in Churches n. 7)

Liturgical Formation

The task of explaining the meaning of the Liturgy and overseeing its correct celebration is an integral part of the Bishop's office of governing the particular Church entrusted to him. Both by word and example the Bishop "should make clear the inherent meaning of the rites and the liturgical texts, and nourish the spirit of the Liturgy in the Priests, Deacons and lay faithful so that they are all led to the active and fruitful celebration of the Eucharist." (RS 22)

Liturgical formation should be available to all: "The Bishop should be determined that the Priests, the Deacons, and the lay Christian faithful grasp ever more deeply the genuine significance of the rites and liturgical texts, and thereby be led to the active and fruitful celebration of the Eucharist." (GIRM 22)

Liturgical catechesis

Already over 150 years ago, the founder of the Liturgical Movement, the Abbot of Solesmes, Dom Prosper Guéranger, was calling for catechesis and wrote that the Liturgy provides, both in content and structure, the best means for teaching the faithful. Guéranger taught that through visible signs, symbols, words and music the mystery which is being celebrated is made present and becomes a source of life for the people of God.

Abbot Guéranger believed that a profound understanding of the Liturgy can only come by studying and meditating upon the texts of the Liturgy. He saw that the task of the liturgist, like that of the scriptural exegete, is to explain the letter of the text in order to reveal its spirit. Guéranger was convinced that the teaching given in the Liturgy is more readily assimilated than many an academic course of study. He considered that the liturgical books are the Church's theological manual. It is, therefore, necessary that priests and people should meditate and reflect upon the texts of the Liturgy.

"The best catechesis on the Eucharist is the Eucharist itself well celebrated" (Benedict XVI)

Abbot Guéranger spoke of the Liturgy as the most solemn and popular form of teaching and he exhorted the bishops of his day to follow the example of the Fathers of the Church and give homilies on the meaning of the Liturgy and the sacred Scriptures. He was convinced to a degree which few people are today of the incomparable value of liturgical catechesis: "who can tell what life giving graces would be poured out on the Christian people, as a direct result of a teaching based upon the explanation and understanding of the mysteries, words and rites of the Liturgy?"

Training for all who have a function in the Liturgy

In the Rule of Saint Benedict it is evident that great care should be taken in the way in which the Liturgy is celebrated. There must be nothing slovenly or perfunctory about the way we celebrate. "The brethren are not to read or sing each in his turn, but those only who give edification to the hearers." For Saint Benedict, to read in the Liturgy is not a right but is the duty and responsibility of those who are capable and have been trained.

Again Saint Benedict insists that: "the intoning of psalms and antiphons shall be done by those who are appointed for it in their order after the abbot. But let no one presume to sing or read, unless he can fulfil the office to the edification of his hearers. Let it be done with humility, gravity, and reverence, and by the one whom the abbot has appointed." Saint Benedict wants the dignity and the beauty of the Liturgy to have first importance and to achieve this requires training and formation.

The same care for what one might call the style of the Liturgy in shown in Saint Benedict's instruction about good order in choir: "Let the brethren, therefore, receive the kiss of peace, go to Communion, intone the psalms, and stand in choir according to the order which the abbot has determined or which they have of themselves." Nothing is to be haphazard.

The Study of the Liturgy

For the student of Liturgy, the liturgical books of the Churches of both the east and the west, those still in use and those no longer in use, are the sources that should be studied. Abbot Guéranger recommended the study of these liturgical books before reading books about the Liturgy. The Abbot of Solesmes admitted that the study of the Liturgical books is not easy, and that at the beginning can sometimes be dry and arid, but that it is a study that brings rich results. Guéranger declared that anyone who studies these sources will become a 'true liturgist' and not a mechanically minded rubricist.

"If the lover of liturgical studies goes to the sources, to the learned commentators, to the various monographs which we have indicated, his progress in the knowledge of doctrine will be quick; but we repeat it again, if anyone should study only the books of the Liturgy, such a one will make progress and in time become a true liturgist and not one of these mechanically minded people who know how to produce a diocesan Ordo but nothing more than that... ." (Prosper Guéranger, Abbot of Solesmes)

The Structure of the Mass

"We must learn to understand the structure of the Liturgy and why it is laid out as it is." (Pope Benedict XVI)

The essential elements in the structure of the Mass have remained unchanged from the time of the Apostles. There have been developments and enrichments in the form of the Mass, but as Pope Benedict remarked, "The liturgy which developed in the course of two millenniums has always remained a continuation of ongoing growth of worship and proclamation."

There are two parts in the Mass that make up one single act of worship: the Liturgy of the Word and the Liturgy of the Eucharist.

The Liturgy of the Word is made up of the proclamation of readings from Holy Scripture, the homily, the Creed (on Sundays and Solemnities) and ends with the Prayer of the Faith or Bidding Prayers.

The Liturgy of the Eucharist begins with the procession and presentation of the bread and wine for the holy Sacrifice. When the Prayer over the Gifts has been said, the celebrant begins the Eucharistic Prayer. After the *Great Amen* at the end of the Eucharistic Prayer, the preparation for Holy Communion begins with the *Our Father* and the prayer for the peace and unity of the Church. While the *Lamb of God* is sung there takes place the ancient and sacred gesture of the 'breaking of the bread'. After Communion and thanksgiving, the Liturgy of the Eucharist is brought to a close with the Prayer after Communion.

As is fitting, these two parts of the Mass, Word and Sacrament, are preceded by an introduction and followed by a conclusion.

The introductory rites are: the Entrance Antiphon and the veneration of the altar followed by the greeting, the Penitential Act, the *Lord, have mercy*, the *Glory to God* (when prescribed) and the Collect Prayer.

The Mass ends with the concluding rites which consist of the final greeting and blessing followed by the dismissal, the veneration of the altar and the final procession.

Once we have grasped the structure of the Liturgy and its various parts, we must make it our own. "We must interiorize the structure, the words of the Liturgy, the Word of God. By doing this, our celebration truly becomes a celebration 'with' the Church: Our hearts are enlarged and we are not doing just anything but are 'with' the Church, in conversation with God." (Pope Benedict XVI)

Enough emphasis has not been laid upon explaining the structure and shape of the Liturgy.

"We must learn to understand the structure of the liturgy and why it is laid out as it is ... To the extent that we have interiorized this structure, comprehended this structure, assimilated the words of the liturgy; we can not only speak to God as individuals, but enter into the 'we' of the Church who is praying. And we thus transform our 'I' in this way, by entering into the 'we' of the Church, enriching and enlarging this 'I', praying with the Church, with the words of the Church, truly being in conversation with God." (*Pope Benedict XVI*)

The Eucharist was celebrated before it was formulated

Nowhere in the Gospels is it recorded that the Lord told his disciples to write things down. He told them to imitate his example, to celebrate his memory and to go out and proclaim the Good News, the Gospel, to the ends of the earth.

From the New Testament writings we can see that the first followers of Jesus thought that the Second Coming was imminent and since the time was short, they did not see the need to write things down. Saint Paul in his letters had to deal with this issue and some of the problems that had arisen because of it. It was only when the Christian community realised that the Apostles and those who had seen the Lord were beginning to disappear from the scene as the years passed, that some recognised the time had come to write down what they had heard.

It is important to keep in mind that the first followers of Jesus celebrated the Liturgy before they formulated it. As Dom Gregory Dix wrote in his now classic study *The Shape of the Liturgy*: "It is important for the understanding of the whole future history of the Liturgy to grasp the fact that Eucharistic worship from the outset was not based on Scripture at all, but solely on tradition. The authority for its celebration was the historical tradition that, it had been instituted by Jesus, cited incidentally by St. Paul and attested in the second Christian generation by the written Gospels." (*The Shape of the Liturgy*, p.3)

Knowledge of the history of the Liturgy is important and helps us to understand not only change and development but also the true nature of tradition. Abbot Guéranger once retorted in exasperation to his critics, "I never said the Liturgy could not change, I have written the history of the development and change which took place through the centuries." Of those who call themselves 'traditionalists' he wrote, "they lack a knowledge of theology, I know, I used to be one of them!"

Guéranger wrote that to think that the Liturgy is unchangeable is "a contradiction of the genius of the Church which enables her to adapt to the needs of the times, and she, like every inhabitant of this world, is subject to the law of salutary progress... The Church, the mystical body of Jesus Christ, is subject to a law of development."

The Participants in the Art of Celebration

"The celebration of the Eucharist is the action of Christ and of the Church, namely, of the holy people united and ordered under the Bishop, who celebrates either in person or through Priests who are his helpers." (GIRM 91)

While recognising that the whole People of God participates in the celebration of the sacred mysteries, Pope Benedict XVI declared that "the art of celebration entails a specific responsibility on the part of those who have received the sacrament of Holy Orders." (*Sacramentum caritatis* 39)

The Priest

"I encourage the clergy always to see their Eucharistic ministry as a humble service offered to Christ and his Church." (Pope Benedict XVI)

The Bishop and his co-worker and collaborator the Priest both act in the name of the whole Church, when presenting to God the prayer of the Church, and above all when offering the Eucharistic sacrifice."

At his ordination the priest is told: "Receive the oblation of the holy people to be offered to God. Understand what you do, imitate what you celebrate, and conform your life to the mystery of the Lord's Cross." Priests do 'seek to understand what they do' and express this in their celebration of the Sacred Mysteries. In recent years this task has become more difficult and complex. Today we live in a society that is very sensitive to the art of communication and high standards are demanded of those who exercise public functions. Those who exercise a ministerial role cannot ignore this fact and 'must pay adequate attention to all of that can enhance the decorum and sacredness of the Eucharistic celebration'. (DLMP 49)

The *Directory on the Life and Ministry of Priests* considers that an understanding of the aesthetic dimension of the art of celebration "can contribute to a better participation in the Eucharistic Sacrifice". On the other hand, neglect of aesthetics can lead to "a lack of attention to the symbolic aspects of the Liturgy and, even more, carelessness and coldness, superficiality and disorder, empty the meaning and weaken the process of strengthening the faith." (DLMP 49)

The dimension of personality

The ability to hold the attention of the congregation and lead them with a charismatic style is regarded in some Christian communities if not an indispensable quality, at least, a very desirable one. While this may not be a problem for a person with a naturally extrovert personality, it can be for those of a more introvert or retiring character. Those of a more reserved temperament can experience difficulties living in an extrovert culture.

While not dealing explicitly with the tension between extrovert and introvert personality, the apostolic exhortation *Sacramentum caritatis* comes close to the problem when it states that: "in their ministry priests must never put themselves or their personal opinions in first place, but Jesus Christ. Any attempt to make themselves the centre of the liturgical action contradicts their very identity as priests. The priest is above all a servant of others, and he must continually work at being a sign pointing to Christ, a docile instrument in the Lord's hands. This is seen particularly in his humility in leading the liturgical assembly, in obedience to the rite, uniting himself to it in mind and heart, and avoiding anything that might give the impression of an inordinate emphasis on his own personality". (*Sacramentum caritatis* 23)

The Deacon

"Let all respect the Deacons as they would Jesus Christ" (St Ignatius of Antioch)

The Deacon is ordained to assist the Bishop and has the responsibility of teaching and administration of church goods, such as providing for the needy. (cf. Acts 6: 1-6)

"Strengthened by sacramental grace, Deacons are dedicated to the People of God, in conjunction with the

Bishop and his body of Priests, in the service of the Liturgy, of the Gospel and of works of charity." (*Lumen gentium* 29)

The Deacon participates in the one ecclesiastical ministry of sacred Orders. The specific sacramental dimension of the Deacon is that of being a sign in the Church of Christ the servant, who came not to be served but to serve and give his life for our salvation.

Service is an essential part of the Church's mission to which all are called and so the Deacon is a permanent reminder of this. The Deacon reminds all Christians of the diaconal aspect of the priesthood of the faithful through baptism.

"It is necessary also that the Deacons, the dispensers of the mysteries of Jesus Christ, be in every way pleasing to all. For they are ... servants of the Church of God." (St Ignatius of Antioch)

While the Deacon "holds first place among those who minister in the celebration of the Eucharist" it is not his liturgical function which is primary. His mission of service should find expression in the Liturgy and not be limited to it.

"At Mass the Deacon has his own part in proclaiming the Gospel, from time to time in preaching God's word, in announcing the intentions of the Universal Prayer, in ministering to the Priest, in preparing the altar and in serving the celebration of the Sacrifice, in distributing the Eucharist to the faithful, especially under the species of wine, and from time to time in giving instructions regarding the people's gestures and posture." (GIRM 94)

"The spirituality of service is a spirituality of the whole Church, insofar as the whole Church, in the same way as Mary, is the 'handmaid of the Lord' (Lk 1: 28), at the service of the salvation of the world. And so that the whole Church may better live out this spirituality of service, the Lord gives her a living and personal sign of his very being as servant. In a specific way, this is the spirituality of the Deacon. In fact, with sacred ordination, he is constituted a living icon of Christ the servant within the Church." (*Directory on the Ministry and Life of Deacons* n. 11)

Married Deacons

"A Deacon must be faithful to his wife and must manage his children and his household well." (1 Tim 3: 12)

Speaking of the permanent diaconate, Pope Benedict XVI declared, "I would like to express my joy and my gratitude for the Council, because it revived this important ministry in the universal Church." The Pope went on to underline "the link between the lay world, the professional world, and the world of the priestly ministry - given that many Deacons continue carrying out their professions and maintain their positions -

important or those of a simple life - while on Saturday and Sunday they work in the Church. In this way, you give witness in the world of today, as well as in the working world, of the presence of faith, of the sacramental ministry and the diaconal dimension of the sacrament of Orders. This seems very important to me: the visibility of the diaconal dimension."

A married Deacon should from time to time participate in the Liturgy with his family. The Deacon should not become so associated with the celibate image of the clergy that the fact that he has received the sacrament of holy matrimony, which represents the union of Christ and his Church, is overshadowed.

An answer to a query published by the Congregation for Divine Worship in its journal *Notitiae* made it clear that the phrase 'a Priest or Deacon' does not imply that "a Deacon may exercise the office of presiding when Priests are present". The mind of the legislator is that the Deacon is ordained to assist the Bishop or Priest. Accordingly, on the basis of the current norms, a Deacon is not to preside at the celebration of the office nor give benediction when Priests are present.

The assembled people of God

"Where two or three are gathered in my name, there am I in the midst of them" (Mt 18: 20)

In describing the functions of the People of God assembled for worship, the *General Instruction of the Roman Missal* affirms that "in the celebration of Mass the faithful form a holy people, a people of God's own possession and a royal priesthood, so that they may give thanks to God and offer the unblemished sacrificial Victim not only by means of the hands of the Priest but also together with him, and so that they may learn to offer their very selves."

This description affirms the sacred and holy character of the worshipping community. This character also carries with it great responsibilities. As the old saying goes, charity begins at home. So the Instruction sees the exercise of charity as being rooted in the gathering of the faithful who, "should, moreover, take care to show this by their deep religious sense and their charity toward brothers and sisters who participate with them in the same celebration".

To preserve charity every effort should be made to avoid any appearance of singularity or division. Each day we pray to our Father and since we have only one Father in heaven it follows that we are all brothers or sisters one to the other.

The unity of the community finds visible expression in various ways especially through gestures and bodily postures. Clearly these should not be performed mechanically and anything that might resemble military precision should be avoided. As Saint Benedict pointed out, discipline helps preserve charity; it also ensures harmony and enhances the dignity of the individual and the assembly. Such a community can be seen "to form one body, whether in hearing the word of God or in taking part in the prayers and in the singing, or above all by the common offering of the Sacrifice and by a participating together at the Lord's Table". (GIRM 96)

Over the past few decades there has been a growing awareness in society of the importance and significance of 'body language'. The fact that the rich tradition of liturgical body language has fallen in some instances into disuse has been a serious impoverishment in the life of Catholics. Liturgical body language helps to express the unity of the community and its active participation in the rite.

Respecting the unity of the worshipping community does not rule out the legitimate diversity of character that can be found in any gathering of the faithful (GIRM 24).

The active participation of the people of God assembled in the Liturgy is rooted in, and an affirmation of, Christ's presence in their midst. "In the celebration of Mass, in which the Sacrifice of the Cross is perpetuated Christ is really present in the very assembly gathered in his name". (GIRM 27)

For many years, Pope Benedict XVI has been emphasising in his writings and teaching that the "Liturgy is not of our 'making' but God's action upon and with us ... Liturgy is a sharing in the Trinitarian dialogue between Father, Son and Holy Spirit." We must not forget, continues the Holy Father, "that the Liturgy is supposed to be God's work, in which he himself acts first, and we become the redeemed precisely because he is at work. The group that celebrates itself celebrates absolutely nothing, because the group is not a reason for celebrating." (*Pope Benedict XVI*)

Pope Saint Pius X promoted active participation in liturgical worship in 1903 in his *Motu proprio* encouraging the singing of Gregorian chant. The importance of participation, especially through singing, was expanded by Pope Pius XII in his encyclical *Mediator Dei*:

"so that the faithful take a more active part in divine worship, ... it is very necessary that the faithful attend the sacred ceremonies not as if they were outsiders or mute onlookers, but let them fully appreciate the beauty of the Liturgy and take part in the sacred ceremonies, alternating their voices with the priest and the choir, according to the prescribed norms. If, please God, this is done, it will not happen that the congregation hardly ever or only in a low murmur answer the prayers in Latin or in the vernacular. A congregation that is devoutly present at the sacrifice, in which our Saviour together with His children redeemed with His sacred blood sings the nuptial hymn of His immense love, cannot keep silent, for - song befits the lover - and, as the ancient saying has it, 'He who sings well prays twice'. (MD 192)

This full, conscious and active participation is not so much a practical directive as a manifestation of the growing theological understanding of the nature of communal worship. Active participation must be understood as a consequence of Baptism, whereby we become members of the People of God, a chosen race, a royal priesthood, a holy nation, a redeemed people (cf. 1 Peter 2: 9; *Lumen gentium*, nn 9-17).

In order that the art of actively taking part in the celebration may become a reality there will always be a need for ongoing formation of the clergy and the faithful. Pope Pius XII recognised this and wrote in his encyclical *Mediator Dei*: "Try in every way, with the means and helps that your prudence deems best, that the clergy and people become one in mind and heart, and that the Christian people take such an active part in the Liturgy that it becomes a truly sacred action of due worship to the eternal Lord in which the priest, chiefly responsible for the souls of his parish, and the ordinary faithful are united together. (MD 199)

Various functions and ministries

"There must then be an adequate preparation. Altar servers must know what to do; lectors must be truly experienced speakers. Then the choir, the singing, should be rehearsed. And let the altar be properly decorated. All this, even if it is a matter of many practical things, is part of the 'art of celebration'" (*Pope Benedict XVI*)

The instituted acolyte

Acolyte means 'one who follows or assists another' and the function came about from a division of the liturgical duties of the diaconal ministry.

Pope Paul VI in the motu proprio *Ministeria quaedam*, (August 15, 1972) described the role of the acolyte at the celebration of Mass as follows: "to aid the Deacon and to minister to the priest at the altar especially at the Preparation of the Gifts and to assist in the distribution of Holy Communion when necessary". The acolyte is also required to instruct others who fulfil functions like carrying the Missal, cross, candles, and other such duties.

When an acolyte is present, he must perform the functions that pertain to his ministry and the excuse for not doing so must not be that it would curtail the participation of other non-instituted servers.

The Lector

The lector is appointed and instituted to fulfil the following functions in the Liturgy: (1) to read the lessons from sacred Scripture, except for the Gospel, in the Mass and other liturgical celebrations; (2) to recite the psalm between the readings when there is no psalmist; (3) to present the intentions for the Bidding Prayers in the absence of the Deacon or cantor; (4) to direct the singing and the participation of the faithful.

The lector also has a role in catechesis for he "may also instruct the faithful for the worthy reception of the sacraments", (and) "take care of preparing other faithful who by a temporary appointment are to read the Scriptures in liturgical celebrations".

The institution of a lector is a reminder that not everyone is capable or suited for fulfilling this function. As Saint Benedict pointed out in the Rule, "The brethren are not to read or sing each in his turn, but those only who give edification to the hearers." (RB 38)

It is inappropriate to allow a person to read who is not fully trained. Poor reading is a mark of disrespect to the assembly and would be unacceptable in other areas of public communication such as broadcasting and various forms of entertainment. Lower standards are not acceptable in church.

Altar servers

The function and indispensable role of those who serve at the altar has a tradition of more than one thousand years. The Synod of Mainz in the ninth century decreed that "Every priest should have a cleric or boy to read the epistle or lesson, to answer him at Mass, and with whom he can chant the psalms."

According to the Code of Canon Law "All lay persons can also perform the functions of commentator or cantor, or other functions, according to the norm of law". (Canon 230, 2)

In an instruction dated June 30, 1992, the Congregation for Divine Worship and the Discipline of the Sacraments declared that "all lay persons" included female altar servers.

While the introduction of this modification was not universally welcomed, the decorum and dignity shown by female servers has been recognised and has in many places improved the quality of this service.

Neither male nor female altar servers should stand at the altar during the celebration of the Eucharist. The priest is assisted at the altar by a Deacon, whose role may not be replaced by a lay minister. They serve at the altar but do not 'stand' at the altar. (GIRM 100)

The psalmist

It is the responsibility of the psalmist to sing the Psalm or canticle, which follow the readings. That this function be carried out correctly, the psalmist is required to have a specific formation in the duties of this ministry, "to be accomplished in the art of singing Psalms and have a facility in public speaking and elocution". (GIRM 102)

The musical ministry

From the first decades of the life of the Church, music has held an honourable place. We find Saint Paul exhorting the faithful to sing psalms, hymns, and canticles of praise (Col 3:16).

There even arose a proverb in praise of singing: "One who sings well prays twice."

The disappearance of many parish choirs in the years following the Second Vatican Council was a great impoverishment to the liturgical life of the Church. There were some who argued erroneously that a choir inhibited the active participation of the assembly, whereas the contrary is the case. A choir is a support to the congregation and fosters the active participation of the faithful by means of singing.

A congregation needs the support of a musical accompaniment. The Church recognises this by allowing the use of an instrument to accompany the singing even during Advent and the penitential period of Lent.

All musical instruments have their beauty and particular characteristic but not all are suitable for large gatherings. Musicians need to be competent and proficient in their art. The musician has a ministerial role. Music is not an aesthetic addition to the Liturgy but contributes to the communication of the word of God and the preaching of the good news of salvation.

"I urge everyone to do their best to take care, also through special liturgical groups, of the preparation and celebration of the Eucharist, so that all who take part in it may encounter the Lord." (Pope Benedict XVI)

Sacristan

The sacristan has a liturgical function but it is one which generally precedes and follows a celebration and for that reason this task is not always given the credit which it merits.

It is the responsibility of the sacristan to ensure that the liturgical books, vestments, water and wine, candles and the many other things that are necessary for the celebration of Mass are prepared and put in their correct place.

The sacristan should ensure that both before after a celebration of the Liturgy, due care and reverence be taken in setting out sacred objects and returning them to their place of safe keeping. It is inappropriate to carry out the Gospel Book as one object among many, after the solemn way in which it was carried at the beginning of the celebration.

Commentator

Given the often heard complaint that there are 'too many words' in a celebration it is not surprising that the explanations and exhortations of a commentator may not always be welcome. The commentator has a delicate task to perform and the remarks and directions that are to be given must not be left to spontaneous comments. The commentator's texts need to be prepared with the same care as a homily. Comments should be very brief and direct the attention of the faithful to the celebration and ensure that they are better disposed for understanding it. The General Instruction asks that the commentator's remarks "should be thoroughly prepared and notable for their restraint".

Those who take up the collection in the church are not simply performing a practical task but are reminding everyone of God's goodness and how he asks of us to share the gifts which he has given us with those in need.

Practical Application of Principles

It is forbidden to introduce elements from other rites or other forms of the Roman Rite, no matter how laudable and edifying they may be. It may never be argued that because a practice is not explicitly forbidden that it may be introduced.

Immediate preparations

All that is needed for the celebration should be prepared and put in place in good time, in an unhurried way, showing proper respect to the altar and the tabernacle. This is a very positive contribution towards creating a recollected atmosphere. When possible the vestments for the Priest, the Deacon, and other ministers should be laid out ready in the sacristy.

Nothing that is used in the Liturgy is insignificant.

The altar is to be covered with at least one white cloth. On or next to the altar are placed candlesticks with lighted candles. A cross adorned with a figure of Christ crucified may be placed on the altar or close to it.

The candles and the cross with the figure of Christ crucified may be carried in the Entrance Procession. If the Gospel Book is not carried in the Entrance Procession it is placed on the altar before Mass. The Lectionary is placed on the ambo and not carried in procession. The Missal and texts that the Priest may need should be put in a convenient place near the chair.

On the credence table are put all the elements needed for the Liturgy of the Eucharist. As a mark of respect, the chalice may be covered with a veil, which may be either of the colour of the day or white.

If water is to be blessed, a suitable jug of water, a small dish of salt and the holy water container and sprinkler are prepared in a suitable place.

The Priest and Deacon should wash their hands on arrival in the sacristy, and other ministers should be encouraged to do the same.

All ministers should take care in vesting, even to the point of making sure that shirt or clerical collars are not visible.

An unhurried start

The Introductory Rites enable the congregation to be of one mind and heart so that all present are ready to listen to word of God and celebrate the holy Eucharist. The ministers, therefore, should wait in silence until the signal is given for the intonation of the Entrance Chant.

The Priest, having put incense into the thurible, blesses it with the Sign of the Cross. The procession to the altar is led by the thurifer followed by the Processional Cross accompanied by candle bearers, other servers follow. The

Deacon carries the Gospel Book walking immediately in front of the priest. Awareness that this procession symbolises the Lord coming among his people, will of itself ensure that this moment is carried out with due solemnity and dignity.

Veneration of the altar

When the Celebrant and the ministers reach the place of celebration, they genuflect if the tabernacle with the Most Blessed Sacrament is situated in the sanctuary. After making a sign of reverence to the altar in the form of a profound bow, the Celebrant and the ordained ministers then venerate the altar with a kiss.

The Celebrant receives the censer from the Deacon or server and incenses the altar.

If the cross is situated on the altar or near it, is incensed by the Priest before he incenses the altar, otherwise, he incenses it when he passes in front of it.

These initial gestures are of great importance and should be carried out unhurriedly. Care must always be taken throughout the Liturgy to avoid anything that might appear affected or artificial. Unity in movement and such details as all bowing at the same time and walking in step does help to create an aspect of good order. Gestures must not be exaggerated. The bowing of the head is a simple gesture but it is often wrongly replaced by a bow of head and shoulders.

60

Sign of the Cross

The opening words and gesture with which the people of
God begin their celebration affirm both their baptismal
profession of faith in God, Father, Son and Holy Spirit
and their mission to witness it before the whole world
(Matthew 28:19; John 14:13-14; Acts 2:21).

The priest alone says "In the name of the Father and of
the Son and of the Holy Spirit" but the Sign of the Cross
is made reverently by all.

The people alone reply "Amen." *Amen* occurs several
times in the Liturgy and always has the meaning of an
affirmative assent to what has been said and
accomplished. The priest does not join in the *Amen*.

Greeting

The community is assembled in the name of Christ Jesus,
"where two or three are gathered in my name, there I am
in their midst" (Mt 18:20). This belief in the Lord's
presence is shown by the greeting and acknowledged by
the people's response. Any form of secular greeting, such
as "good morning", is not to be used since it undermines
the significance of what it means to be assembled in
Christ. If there is a need for a particular word of welcome,
such as at Weddings or Funerals, this takes place after the
greeting and before the introduction to the Mass.

At the beginning of the words of the greeting the priest
has his hands joined and only opens them towards the

people at the words "be with you all". This pattern with the gesture being made at the words "be with you all" should be used with the other greetings in the course of the Liturgy.

After the initial Greeting and before the Penitential Act, the Priest should make a brief introduction to the Mass of the day. If appropriate the Deacon or another person may do this. It is fitting for the Deacon to introduce the Mass on the Feast day of a Deacon, for example, Saint Stephen or Saint Lawrence. A member of a religious Order could introduce the Mass on a founder's or Patron's Feast day and other similar circumstances. No task should be given to another purely on the basis of increasing the number of those who fulfil a function in the celebration. It is the Priest's duty to preside and while he should not usurp the functions of others he must not relinquish any of his responsibilities on the false premise of increasing lay participation.

The Introduction to the Mass is not to be incorporated into the Penitential Act.

The Penitential Act

After the introduction to the Mass of the day, the Priest invites the faithful to participate in a Penitential Act. This is an acknowledgement of our unworthiness so that our hearts and minds may be made ready to celebrate the sacred mysteries.

The text given in this Missal is to be used as it is, since there is no longer a rubric 'in these or similar words'. The Penitential Act is concluded by the priest imploring the Lord's pardon and forgiveness.

Body language, as we said, is important as a form of communication which also enhances and explains verbal communication. Since signs and symbols are such an integral part of the Liturgy, body language, such as striking the breast, has a place in our celebrations.

The act of standing, sitting, bowing and kneeling in a common, unified movement is a sign of dignity and respect both for God and for neighbour. Good posture is encouraged even in secular society as an aid to good health. A healthy liturgical assembly, priest and people, needs to be attentive to posture.

The *Glory to God in the highest* is an ancient and venerable hymn by which the Church, gathered in the Holy Spirit, glorifies and entreats God the Father and the Lamb. The text of this hymn may not be replaced by any other. It is sung or said on Sundays outside Advent and Lent, and also on Solemnities and Feasts, and may be used at particular celebrations to give a more solemn character.

The Collect

These presidential prayers are so called because the Priest who presides over the assembly in the person of Christ, addresses God in the name of the entire holy people and of all present.

The words "Let us pray" are said with hands joined. All pray silently with the Priest for a brief moment. With hands extended, the Priest sings or says the Collect, at the end of which the people acclaim: "Amen."

All 'presidential' prayers must be spoken or sung in an audible and clear voice if the faithful are to listen attentively. It is unacceptable that a priest prays the Collect, Prayer over the Gifts and Prayer after Communion without having first read them privately and meditated upon their contents. The faithful, too, should be encouraged to become familiar with these prayers which will provide rich nourishment for their spiritual life.

The Liturgy of the Word

When all are seated, the Priest may, very briefly, introduce the faithful to the Liturgy of the Word. Such an introduction needs to be well prepared and preferably written down so that it is succinct and does not turn into a pre-homily.

The readings

The readings from the word of God are to be listened to reverently by everyone, for they are an element of the greatest importance in the Liturgy. The faithful should sit during the readings before the Gospel, during the Responsorial Psalm and for the Homily.

The manner of pronouncing the different texts

Training for reading is indispensable and the standard of public reading in church must be equal to that required in other walks of life. No one is to be asked to read who is not up to the task. At a marriage or a funeral care should be taken that a family member or friend who may not be accustomed to reading in church be given adequate preparation.

The tone, pitch of voice and style must be fitted to the nature of the reading, but dramatic or theatrical effects should be avoided. The text must not be 'interpreted' by the reader using too subjective a style or placing an undue emphasis on certain words. The singing of the texts, especially the Gospel, is an effective means towards an objective proclamation.

Professional training should be available to all: Priest, Deacon, reader and everyone who is called upon to address the congregation.

Words such as 'say' and 'proclaim' are to be understood either of singing or of reciting.

When the Responsorial Psalm cannot be sung, it should be read slowly and attention given to its poetical character and rhythm. There should be no need for the reader to begin by saying "the response is". This is an indication that the reader presumes that the structure of the Responsorial Psalm is not understood after nearly forty years of use!

In a sung Mass, texts from the repertoire of Gregorian chants given in the *Graduale Romanum* may be used.

The Gospel

The ceremonial and marks of honour that accompany the proclamation of the Gospel show that this is the most sacred moment of the Liturgy of the Word. The one who is to proclaim the Gospel makes a special preparation. The Deacon receives a Blessing so that he may proclaim the Gospel 'worthily and well'. In the absence of a Deacon, the Priest prepares himself by bowing before the altar and saying quietly, "Cleanse my heart and my lips, almighty God, that I may worthily proclaim your holy Gospel."

In a solemn celebration, the Gospel Book is carried in procession to the place of its proclamation accompanied by candles and incense. Such marks of reverence help to prepare the minds and hearts of all present as they stand to listen to the holy reading.

"When the Gospel is to be read at Mass, stand up to show that you are ready and equipped to walk on the way that the Gospel commands." (Saint Francis de Sales)

At the ambo, the Priest or Deacon opens the book and, with hands joined, says: "The Lord be with you." The hands are joined because this is not a presidential greeting but rather in the nature of an affirmation of the presence of the Lord.

While announcing the passage of the Gospel to be read, the Deacon or Priest makes the Sign of the Cross on the book and on his forehead, lips, and breast, which everyone else does as well. This outward gesture expresses the desire that the words of the holy Gospel should be in our mind, in our mouth, and in our heart. The Gospel Book is then reverenced with incense.

At the end of the proclamation of the Gospel, the Deacon, or the Priest, acclaims: "The Gospel of the Lord", and all reply: "Praise to you, Lord Jesus Christ." These words declare that we believe that through the power of the Holy Spirit, the Lord is present to us in the proclamation of the Gospel. The kissing of the book is not only a sign of reverence but an acknowledgement of the presence of the Holy Spirit. The proclamation of the Gospel is always a call to conversion, "repent and believe in the Gospel" and so the kissing of the book is accompanied by the words, "Through the words of the Gospel may our sins be wiped away."

It is a serious abuse for the Deacon or Priest to place the Gospel Book on a shelf under the ambo or in any other unfitting place. After the solemnity that precedes the reading of the Gospel, it is more than incongruous to give the impression of discarding the Gospel Book.

The homily

It is in the homily that the preacher breaks the bread of the Word of God for the nourishment of the faith of the Christian community. The one who gives the homily teaches in the name of the Church and serves the living tradition of the Church.

"The homily is a means of bringing the scriptural message to life in a way that helps the faithful to realize that God's word is present and at work in their everyday lives. It should lead to an understanding of the mystery being celebrated, serve as a summons to mission, and prepare the assembly for the profession of faith, the universal prayer and the Eucharistic Liturgy." (*Pope Benedict XVI*)

It is because preaching in the Catholic Church is very often limited to the homily at Mass that the true form and nature of a homily is being distorted. Of course sound doctrine and moral teaching must be given but the homily does not always lend itself as the most suitable vehicle for this. This is a pastoral problem which needs to be examined.

Those who are to preach the Word of God should "cultivate a knowledge of Holy Scripture with a sound exegesis, principally patristic, and meditated on according to the various methods supported by the spiritual tradition of the Church, in order to obtain a living understanding of love. Seen in this light, the priest will feel the duty of paying particular attention to the preparation, be it remote or proximate, of liturgical homilies, to their content, to the balance between the theoretical and practical aspects, to the manner of teaching and to the technique of delivery, even to good diction, respectful of the dignity of the matter and of the listeners." (DLMP 47)

A homily which is not prepared is a grave dereliction of duty and those who claim that they rely on the inspiration of the Holy Spirit are acting with presumption.

The Creed: Profession of Faith

At the end of the Homily, the Profession of Faith, when prescribed, is either sung or said. At the words "by the Holy Spirit was incarnate and became man" a profound bow is to be made except on the Solemnities of the Annunciation and of the Nativity of the Lord, when all genuflect at these words.

The Universal Prayer or Prayer of the Faithful or Bidding Prayers

The Universal Prayer, or Prayer of the Faithful (also known as the Bidding Prayers), is of ancient origin. Saint Paul wrote to Timothy that there should be "prayers, petitions, intercessions and thanksgiving for all: for rulers and all in authority, so that we may be able to live quiet and peaceful lives in the full practice of religion and of morality." (1 Timothy 2: 1-4)

These prayers are called the Prayer of the Faithful because in the ancient Church they were begun after the departure of the Catechumens and those who were not yet baptised. In this prayer only the baptised Faithful took part and exercise their priestly function by interceding for the needs of all of humanity.

The Priest, standing at the chair with his hands joined, calls upon the faithful to participate in the Bidding Prayers. Attention must be given to ensure that this invitation is not itself formulated as a prayer. The Deacon, cantor, reader, or another person announces the intentions from the ambo or from some other suitable place.

The individual intentions should not be in the form of a prayer nor be addressed to the Lord. The intention is simply information given to the assembly, who make it their own in prayer.

At the very end, the Priest, with hands extended, concludes the petitions with a prayer.

The prayer which concludes the Bidding Prayers also marks the end of the Liturgy of the Word.

The Liturgy of the Eucharist
- the Presentation of the Gifts

The Liturgy of the Eucharist begins with the Preparation of the Gifts. This rite should not be seen as an "interval" between the Liturgy of the word and the Liturgy of the Eucharist.

"This humble and simple gesture is very significant: in the bread and wine that we bring to the altar, all creation is taken up by Christ the Redeemer to be transformed and presented to the Father. In this way we also bring to the altar all the pain and suffering of the world, in the certainty that everything has value in God's eyes. God invites us to participate in bringing to fulfilment his handiwork, and in so doing, gives human labour its authentic meaning, since, through the celebration of the Eucharist, it is united to the redemptive sacrifice of Christ." (*Pope Benedict XVI*)

When all are seated, the Offertory chant begins and the Deacon assisted by an acolyte or other minister places the corporal, the purificator, the chalice, the pall, and the Missal on the altar.

The faithful express their participation by making an offering and bringing forward bread and wine for the celebration of the Eucharist. An empty chalice must not form part of the procession, the chalice is at the altar to receive the wine which is brought up. This moment of the Liturgy needs careful preparation as it easily risks having an appearance of being a little chaotic. Moments such as this in the Liturgy may need to be practised periodically to ensure that they are carried out with dignity.

The directive which states that the priest raises the paten and the chalice slightly above the altar needs to be respected. If the elements are raised too high the gesture risks becoming an elevation and any such impression must be avoided.

If incense is used, the Priest puts some in the thurible, blesses it silently and incenses the offerings, the cross, and the altar. While standing at the side of the altar, a minister incenses the Priest and then the people.

The washing of the hands must not be reduced to the fingertips. A suitable jug and basin and small towel should be used. The very term 'a finger towel' is indicative of how this rite of washing the hands was reduced to a token gesture.

The Priest extends his hands at the words "Pray, brethren (brothers and sisters)" and then closes them as he continues "that my sacrifice and yours may be acceptable to God, the almighty Father."

The distinction "my sacrifice and yours" is because the priest acts in the person of Christ, not in his own name, and at the same time the people exercise their priesthood, which is different but complementary. Concelebrants do not join in this response of the faithful.

The Prayer over the Gifts concludes the rite of preparation.

The Eucharistic Prayer

"The Eucharistic Prayer is the centre and summit of the entire celebration. The different Eucharistic Prayers contained in the Missal have been handed down to us by the Church's living Tradition and are noteworthy for their inexhaustible theological and spiritual richness."
(Pope Benedict XVI)

Only the Priest in virtue of his Ordination is permitted to proclaim the Eucharistic Prayer. The people participate through the responses in the Preface dialogue, the Holy, Holy, Holy, the acclamation after the Consecration and the acclamation Amen after the concluding doxology. Throughout the prayer the people are one with the Priest with whom they have lifted up their hearts to the Lord in thanksgiving. When appropriate the Priest should sing those parts of the Eucharistic Prayer for which musical notation is provided.

"The recitation of the Eucharistic Prayer requires a moment of special attention if it is to be spoken in such a way that it involves others. I believe we should also find opportunities in catechesis, in homilies and in other circumstances to explain this Eucharistic Prayer well to the People of God so that they can follow the important moments — the account and the words of the Institution, the prayer for the living and the dead, the thanksgiving to the Lord and the epiclesis — if the community is truly to be involved in this prayer." (*Pope Benedict XVI*)

During the Eucharistic Prayer, the Deacon stands near the Priest, but slightly behind him, so that when necessary he may assist the Priest with the chalice or the Missal.

From the epiclesis until the Priest shows the chalice, the Deacon usually remains kneeling. If several Deacons are present, one of them may place incense in the thurible for the Consecration and incense the host and the chalice at the elevation.

Naming in the Eucharistic Prayer

Auxiliary Bishops may be mentioned in the Eucharistic Prayer, but not other Bishops who happen to be present. When several are to be mentioned, this is done with the collective formula: N., our Bishop and his assistant Bishops.

"The words 'with our Holy Father Pope N. and our Bishop N.' are a requisite part of the Church's Eucharistic Prayer. These words are not an addendum of sorts, but a necessary expression of what the Eucharist really is. Furthermore, we mention the Pope and the Bishop by name: unity is something utterly concrete, it has names. In this way unity becomes visible; it becomes a sign for the world and a concrete criterion for ourselves." (*Pope Benedict XVI*)

Use of a bell

A little before the Consecration, if appropriate, a minister rings a small bell as a signal to the faithful. The minister also rings the small bell at each elevation by the Priest, according to local custom. If incense is being used, when the host and the chalice are shown to the people after the Consecration, a minister incenses them.

After the Consecration when the Priest has said: "The mystery of faith", the people pronounce the Acclamation, using one of the prescribed formulas. The Priest does not join in the Acclamation, even under the pretext of sustaining it. Likewise Concelebrants do not join in these Acclamations, which are proper to the people.

At the end of the Eucharistic Prayer, the Priest takes the paten with the host and the chalice and elevates them both while pronouncing alone the doxology. At the end the people acclaim Amen. After this, the Priest places the paten and the chalice on the corporal.

If a Deacon or a concelebrating priest is present, he raises the chalice. No more than one chalice and one paten are ever to be elevated.

After the Eucharistic Prayer is concluded, the Priest, with hands joined, says the introduction to the Lord's Prayer, and then with hands extended, he prays the Lord's Prayer together with the people.

Sign of peace

The Priest announces the greeting of peace, saying: "The peace of the Lord be with you always." His hands are joined and only extended towards the people at the words *be with you always*.

The Deacon or in his absence the Priest says: "Let us offer each other the sign of peace."

The Priest gives the Sign of Peace to the ministers but always remains within the sanctuary, so that the celebration is not disrupted.

Only if there is a reasonable cause should he offer the Sign of Peace to a small number of the faithful. According to what is has been decided by the Conference of Bishops, all express to one another peace, communion, and charity.

While the Sign of Peace is being given, it is permissible to say: "The peace of the Lord be with you always", to which the reply is "Amen." No other forms of greeting or well wishing are to be used. The members of the congregation should avoid leaving their places to exchange the sign of peace.

Communion

When the singing of the *Lamb of God* has begun, the Priest takes the host, breaks it over the paten, and places a small piece in the chalice, saying quietly the accompanying prayer.

Then, with hands joined, he says quietly the prayer for Communion. By not saying aloud these and other prayers that are to be said quietly, he is showing respect for the silent preparation being made by the other members of the assembly.

The Priest genuflects, takes the host but without holding the two broken portions matched together, as this undermines the symbolism of the bread broken for us. The host is to be slightly raised above the paten or above the chalice and any impression of this being a further elevation must be avoided.

While the Priest is receiving the Sacrament, the Communion chant begins.

The Priest then takes the paten or ciborium and approaches the communicants, who should approach in procession, remembering that they are the pilgrim People of God being nourished on their journey. The sacred gifts are *given* and therefore it is not permitted for the faithful to take the consecrated Bread or the sacred chalice by themselves and, still less, to hand them on from one to another among themselves. The faithful communicate either standing or kneeling. An appropriate sign of reverence should be made before receiving the Sacrament.

If Communion is given only under the species of bread, the Priest raises the host slightly and shows it to each, saying: "The Body of Christ." The communicant replies "Amen", and receives the Sacrament either in the hand or on the tongue, the choice lying with the communicant. As soon as the communicant receives the host, he or she consumes the whole of it.

When Communion is given under both kinds, the rite prescribed rite is to be followed. The communicant may not dip the consecrated host into the chalice.

If there are a large number of communicants the Priest can be assisted by other Priests who are present. When a Deacon is present he is the ordinary minister of the chalice. He is not to depute this task to another. When necessary, the Priest may call upon extraordinary ministers to assist him.

The extraordinary minister should not be seen as another form of distributing a part of the Liturgy to others. It should be remembered that these and other functions are not an inherent sign of full and active participation, as this would exclude those who for one reason or another are not able to perform such a function. Moreover, when there is only a small number of communicants, or where sufficient Priests or Deacons are present, extraordinary ministers should not function.

The extraordinary ministers must not approach the altar before the Priest has received Communion, and as a sign of their service to the people they are always to receive from the hands of the Priest celebrant the vessel containing the species of the Most Holy Eucharist for distribution to their brothers and sisters in Christ.

When the distribution of Communion is over, the Priest himself immediately and completely consumes at the altar any consecrated Wine that happens to remain; as for any consecrated hosts that are left, he either consumes them at the altar or carries them to the place designated for the reservation of the Eucharist.

Upon returning to the altar, the Priest collects the fragments, should any remain, and he stands at the side of the altar or at the credence table and purifies the paten or ciborium over the chalice, and dries the chalice with a purificator. If the vessels are purified at the altar, they are carried to the credence table by a minister.

If there is a just need, the vessels needing to be purified may be left on a corporal, suitably covered, and purified immediately after Mass.

The Priest returns to the chair. A sacred silence may now be observed for some time, or a Psalm or other canticle of praise or a hymn may be sung.

Standing at the chair with hands joined, the Priest says: Let us pray; then, with hands extended, he sings or says the Prayer after Communion. A brief period of silence may precede the prayer, unless this has been already observed immediately after Communion. At the end of the prayer the people acclaim: Amen.

The Concluding Rites

When the Prayer after Communion is concluded, if there are any announcements they should be made at this moment. They should be brief, not a rambling list.

After greeting the people in the usual way the Priest, joining his hands again and then immediately placing his left hand on his breast, raises his right hand and says: "May Almighty God bless you". He then makes the Sign of the Cross over the people as he says: "the Father, and the Son, and the Holy Spirit".

On certain days and occasions, this blessing may be given in a more solemn form by a Prayer over the People or another more solemn formula.

A Bishop blesses the people with the appropriate formula, making the Sign of the Cross three times over the people.

Immediately after the Blessing, with hands joined, the Deacon or the Priest dismisses the assembly with one of the prescribed formulas.

The Priest and the Deacon venerate the altar with a kiss and, after he and the ministers have made a profound bow to the altar, and a genuflection to the Blessed Sacrament if present on the sanctuary all withdraw in an orderly manner without other gestures such as shaking hands with members of the congregation. Such signs of fellowship should be given at the church door according to custom.

On those occasions when another liturgical action follows the Mass, the Concluding Rites, that is, the Greeting, the Blessing, and the Dismissal, are omitted.

Conclusion

The *General Instruction of the Roman Missal* provides the most complete guide to the celebration of Mass. It is hoped that this short work will encourage the reader to examine that document which is both practical and rich in theological and liturgical teaching.

"Genuine beauty springs from a perfect harmony of truth and charity which is capable of awakening admiration, wonder and true joy in the hearts of all."
(Pope Benedict XVI)